Research Methodology. A Guide for a Literature Review

A short Description

Farwis Mahrool

Bibliographic information published by the German National Library:

The German National Library lists this publication in the National Bibliography; detailed bibliographic data are available on the Internet at http://dnb.dnb.de.

ISBN: 9783346281890
This book is also available as an ebook.

© GRIN Publishing GmbH
Nymphenburger Straße 86
80636 München

Print and binding: Books on Demand GmbH, Norderstedt, Germany
Printed on acid-free paper from responsible sources.

The present work has been carefully prepared. Nevertheless, authors and publishers do not incur liability for the correctness of information, notes, links and advice as well as any printing errors.

GRIN web shop: https://www.grin.com/document/947576

A Guide for

Literature Review

By:

Mahrool Farwis

PhD- Scholar

Table of Contents

Literature Review

1. What is Literature review?

Literature review is commonly using term in research world and key component of any research work. In literature review, there are two words available, which are literature and review. The word literature commonly known as pieces of writing that are valued as works. Meantime, review means the comparative study or analysing the past available information. So the word literature review its self has the meaning of comparative analysis of past or existing piece of written work. There are many definition advanced by many authors. The common understanding for literature review is a critical assessment by the researcher of the prevailing body of knowledge on the theme or problem under inquiry. Further, as cited by Uma and Roger (2016) literature review is "the collection of existing documents (both published and unpublished) on the topic, which comprise information, ideas, data and evidence written from a specific standpoint to fulfill certain aims or express certain views on the nature of the topic and how it is to be examined, and the effective evaluation of these documents in relation to the research being proposed" (Hart, 1998). This definition has included several concept which comes under literature review. Literature review gives the current and updated knowledge about the study phenomenon. Literature review permits the researchers to enter into a critical engagement with the existing theories, concepts, analysis, information and relevant authors.

Saunders, Lewis and Thornhill (2009) cited in their book that "There is little point in reinventing the wheel . . . the work that you do is not done in a vacuum, but builds on the ideas of other people who have studied the field before you. This requires you describe what has been published, and to marshal the information in a relevant and critical way" Based on this understanding, available scholarly works and previous contribution of researchers for relevant problem must be reviewed through critical literature review. The scholarly investigation finding will certainly be judged in relation to other researchers' study and their outcomes. Therefore, it is required both to 'map and assess the present academic knowledge' to finding out what study has been carried out in selected area, and if possible, to try to identify any other research that might presently be in progress. As a result, the phenomenon under study will enhance your issue's knowledge and aid you to explain research question(s) further (Tranfield et al., 2004).

As per Bakare (2013) literature review means reviews academic work, books, and other causes pertinent to a certain topic, area of research, theoretical background, and by doing that, furnishing an explanation, summary, and critical evaluation of these research. Further he explained that, literature review expose a summary sources which researcher gone through while doing research and prove to your readers how researcher study fits into the larger field of study. So in general, literature review demonstrate a starting point for existing knowledge of a study. In any research work, literature review deliver the justification for the study by sequence study of passed work which will enable to establish the research gap. Literature review is laying foundation to compos background of study, problem statement and purpose of the study. Following that methodological fitness could be justified through past study support (Rocco & Plakhotnik, 2009). Sometime the explanation given for literature review is in a different perspective for instance, Merriam and Simpson (2000) and Tonette and Rocco (2009) highlights that literature review is carried out for the formation of a conceptual frame work or to discover a relevant zone for research. Likewise, a literature review is a portion of the research work, it comprises evidence that provides an idea of the theoretical works that you take as the root for your study (Get-thesis, 2019). Before starting research researchers need to understand what had been done before. They also recognized the importance of scholar being able to acknowledge past research connected to their study to support the scientific process of aggregate research that builds upon prior research (John, Rose & Frank, 2018). Therefore literature review is guiding the researcher from introduction to draw the conclusion of the study.

1.1 Purpose of literature review

John et al (2018) identified the following key purposes that a literature review should provide to research:

- It sets the comprehensive background of the study.
- It clearly defines what is and what is not within the limit of the examination.
- It positions a current literature in a broader scholarly and historical situation.

As per Uyangoda (2010) purposes of literature review identified in five main point one is facilitate the researcher to recognize gaps in the present body of knowledge. It mean addressing a knowledge gap is the main element of research objective. Therefore, literature review furnish the way to identify the prevailing knowledge gap. In order to justify the research gap and stressing knowledge gap, possible only through review of existing body of knowledge. Second purpose is literature review enable the researcher to make sure that the study is a new contribution to knowledge. Which emphzise that a sound study is anticipated to give a brand-new contribution to the existing body of knowledge. A fresh contribution stands that the study is not replication or reinventing the wheel rather it seeks new facts, a new explanation or new theory building. Even though the issue of the study has been subjected to previous research. This objective could be achieved through review of up-to-date studies. Third one is literature review shows familiarity of the researcher with the most up-to-date scholarly work relevant to the theme of the research. Comprehensive literature review enable the reader and evaluator to make sure the study is updated with the latest subject knowledge. To achieve this goal, the researcher shows the ability in critically engage with contemporary scholarly work which is possible by literature review of latest scholar work. Fourth propose is literature review help to frame foundation for the research work. Effective literature review helps to formulate research problem, research question even research method. By referring others scholarly work offers valuable acumens, guidance and direction to the study.

Saunders et al (2009) shows two specific purpose for literature review. One is literature review helps to ascertain theories and thoughts that will guide you to develop theoretical or conceptual framework for the particular research process. Second point is effective literature review enable the researcher to develop theories from the past knowledge.

1.2 Types of literature review

- *Systematic Review* is a synthesis of the available research and experiment which concentrate on a specific research problem. This type of review helps the researcher to overcome likely biases by adopting some method.
- *Meta-analysis* is pools the findings of numerous systematic studies and statistically investigates them. This helps to predetermine the finding of similar research hence on a principle that related studies will have a common truth.
- *Integrative Review* is to be one of the broadest methodological approach of analyses. It comprises theoretical literature, experimental and non-experimental researches. I could be used to outline ideas, analyze issues and examine theories.

This types of literature review advanced by De Souza (2010).

1.3 Structure of sound literature review

Saunders et al (2009) proposes a structure which enable the researcher and reader to understand the past literature at a glance. The critical review of literature structure firstly focus on how far current published study goes in replying the research question(s). Secondly when doing critical review the past studies in which extend relate to our research objectives. Uyangoda (2010) describes the structure under five stages. One is Categorize and cluster literature under review according to proper concept. Second is find strength and inadequacies of present literature by referring summary. Third is organize and arrange the review thematically. Next is note the strength and weakness and GAPS in present knowledge on the theme of the research. Finally justify how particular study expects to fill those knowledge gaps. The sound literature review must consist and follow either way to be the best piece of research.

2. Function of Literature Review

A literature review principally has three functions. First to deliver to the reader what knowledge and ideas have been recognized on a subject, and what their strengths and lacking part in the particular theme of the research. Second function is when undertaking so, obviously convey the concept to the reader that the researcher's awareness with theories and concept. As a result, the reader may think that you're a better scholar compare with experts in the subject field. The common final function is to present the ideas in a specific problem and the theories for to support the phenomenon. (Schrijven, 2017).

Further, there are many sub function of literature review.

- *Provide the context for research*: By reviewing past study, the need for further analysis might highlighted by researchers. This juncture serve as starting point for context for research.
- *Confess the work of others*: In any research work literature review shows the acknowledgement of previous researchers contribution in the relevant theme of investigation and this is the place where others work highlighted, giving due diligence of acknowledgment.
- *Familirse researcher with the field of study:* By referring passed available knowledge enable the researcher to become expert in the field and make familiar with the study field.

- *Notify and amend your own research:* Critical review of literature helps to inform to the reader about authenticity of the researcher contribution.

As per Uma and Roger (2016), a critical review of the literature guide the researcher to find out the wide-range understanding of particular concept, meaning of phenomenon, formulation of conceptual framework, instruments, and analytical tools for respective research theme. Further they emphasized that a review of the literature helps researcher to formulate a theoretical background which will provide comprehensive understanding of relevant subject. Furthermore, earlier related research finding, methodological issues and foremost conclusion of the past studies and latest finding furnish updated knowledge on the topic. Next function is review of the literature uses to the researcher to formulate theoretical background, which allowing scholar to identify the relevant variables that are related to the study. As a result conceptual framework would be established for pertinent study. Based on the past literate, relationship between variables identified and tools for measurement also could be operationalist to find the solution for the specific research problems. Literature review helps researcher to construct the arguments for the relationship between variables which lead to formulate conceptual model. In addition to that, hypothesis can be generated through conceptual model.

The literature review   paly main five functions: (a) to build a foundation, (b) to demonstrate how a study advances knowledge, (c) to conceptualize the study, (d) to assess research design and instrumentation, and (e) to provide a reference point for interpretation of findings. It could further explain that building a foundation requires using prior research in such a way as to validate connections, show trends, and deliver an outline of an idea, theory, or literature base. Next function is demonstrating how any study advances knowledge uses the works to present prevailing knowledge construct a situation that clearly depicts the gap in what is known that a study will address. The common function of conceptualizing a study arises by describing hypothesis and propositions of preceding studies, defining terms, and clarifying assumptions and limitations citing relevant work to build a rationale for a study. Another function of this section of a manuscript is to provide support for the research design, method, and instruments to be used in a study. This is done by making a case for the method the researcher believes appropriate and by illustrating why other methods are not appropriate, citing related work. The last function is to provide a reference point the findings can be compared with and the implications connected to this previously presented work. (Merriam & Simpson, 2000; Tonette & Rocco, 2009).

BEI GRIN MACHT SICH IHR WISSEN BEZAHLT

- Wir veröffentlichen Ihre Hausarbeit,
  Bachelor- und Masterarbeit

- Ihr eigenes eBook und Buch -
  weltweit in allen wichtigen Shops

- Verdienen Sie an jedem Verkauf

Jetzt bei www.GRIN.com hochladen und kostenlos publizieren

Bibliografische Information der Deutschen Nationalbibliothek:

Die Deutsche Bibliothek verzeichnet diese Publikation in der Deutschen National-
bibliografie; detaillierte bibliografische Daten sind im Internet über http://dnb.d-
nb.de/ abrufbar.

Impressum:

Copyright © 2019 GRIN Verlag
Druck und Bindung: Books on Demand GmbH, Norderstedt Germany
ISBN: 9783346057600

Dieses Buch bei GRIN:

https://www.grin.com/document/507110

Martin (2016) explain some important function for literature review: First researcher familiarity with the literature which is straightly pertinent to the topic matters. Without referring of available source for particular phenomenon that could misguide and cheat reader proclaiming that this is the evidence. Secondly for adaptation of theory and framework there are several available in relevant theme of the research. So, literature review guides which is most appropriate for the relevant study. Third function is critical review helps the authors to compare the studies finding in relation with country, industry and context. This aid the author to construct the similarities, differences and further advancement in the relevant field of study. This helps to find out the gap in the knowledge.

Singh (2006) highlighted five key function of literature review. Which are listed here,

1. *The conceptual frame of reference:* By doing literature review, it gives idea to formulate conceptual framework for the research. This is the basic activity to understand the knowledge in the field form past to contemporary. This is the phase where researcher could understand the relevant field of knowledge comprehensively. This compression moderate the researcher mind set in to his/her own view point towards a research problem. Literature review furnish the relevant information for particular research problem with different perspective and context. So this function help to the researcher to understand deep prevailing knowledge which help to formulate the research framework for the particular problem.

2. *Status of Research:* Literate review gives answers for some question which are crucial for critical evaluation. It facilitate the scholar to understand **what** have been studied in the relevant research problem. This are helps the researcher to avoid reinventing the wheel risk. Next it provides **when** this study has happened. Hence, to get recent knowledge latest studies to be reviewed. Sometime old studies may not reflect the current trend of the study problem. Very important aspect is **where** this study done. This is demarcate the context of the study either geographical location, developed and developing countries perspective, urban and rural context and region. To generalize the finding, context must take in to consideration. Past literature show that **who** is the population of the study. Which could further shows the evidence to further studies. Through the review of literature scholar get the glue of **how** study conducted. By this answer, researcher get the status of the research.

3. *Research Approach, Method, Instrumentation and Data Analysis:* Reviewing past literature enable the researcher to adopt research approach. The justification given by the past author also could replicate in your study. Method also same concept which can be applicable as prior research method. Some time, researcher try with another method by

considering the lack of new method applied in past studies. This would help the scholar to justify the methodological gap. As far as instrumentation concern, past studies pave the path to construct the instruments for the same research problem. Evaluating past studies return the tools to the researcher for his/her study are. Data analysis could be undertaken with the guidance of the prior research finding.

4. *Probability of Success and Significance of Findings:* After reviewed of past literature, researcher would come up with the clear picture of prior researcher's unsuccessful implementation of research procedures. So, past studies significant may distorted one beyond the intended outcome. Therefore, new researcher would use another method and use appropriate instruments, through that he/she may achieve the success and study will contribute significantly.

5. *Definitions, Assumptions, Limitations, and Hypotheses:* By reasonable reading, researchers understand the definitions of concept, assumption of the phenomena, limitation and through that hypothesis would established.

Hence, it is clear that literature review functioning as a core in any research project.

3. Empirical and Theoretical Review

There are number of review prevailing in the scholarly world. However empirical and theoretical review pay more attention academic research. Academician must have hand full of knowledge to perform empirical and theoretical review to study the problematic phenomenon. This section explains the definition of empirical and theoretical review and differences between those two reviews.

3.1 Theoretical Review

What is Theory?

Before discussing the theoretical review, try to know what is all about theory. A theory either forecasts or clarifies a phenomenon. As per Dubin (1978) Theories are created by the human mind to comprehend our nature. Theories are required "to satisfy an every human 'need' to order the experienced world. The only instrument employed in the ordering process is the human mind and the 'magic' of human perception and thought". Further, Lynham (2002a) explained that theories are assist human to "understand, explain, anticipate, know, and act. In literature there are many definitions available for theory. However, theory explain the human and environment behavior, through that scholar could predict and understand the human and environment reaction. So, theory guiding about existing knowledge and predicts the future too.

As technology advances through scientific discipline grows, the set of knowledge also grows. Sometime this advances challenge the applicability of formal and informal theories. Therefore, theories become critical for application and explanation of current phenomena. On this context, the researchers need to analyze successive incremental knowledge and obstacles in applying in current context (John, Rose & Frank, 2018). However, theory only giving foundation for the research context phenomenon. So, theory is the core driver for doing scientific research. Theoretical foundation giving back for conceptual framework formulation. Therefore, particular theory must be selected in order to guide the construction of variables. Sometime inappropriate theories also could be selected, as a results deficiencies arises. This may arise due to theory chosen without considering what has been tested, verified, or falsified. Connelly (2014) highlighted this by stating, "When research results are not what were expected, two reasons are possible: either the research design or measurement of variables was imperfect, or the theory directing the research did not appropriate the context". In theoretical literature review, scholars trying to figure out the theories which applied by the past authors to construct particular theme. Consequently, to select the appropriate theory researcher must review the theoretical literature to locate the specific theory for his/her study.

The aim of theoretical review is to study the depth of theory that has gathered in respect to a problem, idea, theory and phenomena. The theoretical literature review aids find what theories already exist, the association between those theories, to what extent the available theories have been studied, and to develop new hypotheses to be established to test the particular research problem (Bakare, 2013). A theoretical review must be incorporated in all research work. Because before starting the research problem, researchers need to recognize which are the existing theories elaborate the concept and phenomenon clearly. Therefore, it is necessary to discuss theories and framework which is pertinent to the particular research problem and how the theories constructed the variables and guides the relationship among them. So that, a theoretical literature review, analyses the theoretical literature underlying on a specific issues. Further, a theoretical literature review is looking at theories which prevailing, how these relate to each other, whether those theories need further investigation, it sure that further studies to validate the relationship. Even though theoretical review has some limitation. Often, selected theories may not reflect the emerging and contemporary research problem. Therefore, usage of the theory become

3.2 Empirical Review

Empirical review contains of an outline of prevailing finding, relevant to a specific research question. The results found out in the past studies with the systematic standardized method to analyses the data in order to draw the conclusion of the research (Bakare, 2013). Empirical review called as systematic review. It examine the past empirical research in order to answer pertinent study question. Empirical studies normally has large sampling size and systematic approach, which may the results of the same theme shows contradicting results. So, researchers show the combing research finding and justify the gap for undertaking the research. Hence, empirical literature review analyses the studies that have been done on specific topic. Furthermore, academic research is based on empirical data, either it could be quantitative or qualitative in nature. In empirical literature, it review the evidences based on actual scientific testing, which could be repeated by someone else to check that the results are accurate.

Characteristics of empirical literature review:

Three characteristics core in empirical literature compared to other types of review.

Systematic Observation and Methodology. In empirical literature, recognized research methodologies and processes are systematically employed to answer the particular research question.

Objectivity. Researchers of empirical literature are anticipated to report the facts as detected, whether or not these facts support the researcher's original hypotheses. Enquiry reliability demands that the evidence be provided in an objective manner, reducing sources of researcher bias to the highest possible level.

Transparency and Replicability/Reproducibility. Empirical literature is reported in such a manner that other researchers understand exactly what was done and what was found in a particular research study. This finding would be reproduced when repeated the study. The results of an original and repetition study may differ, but a reader could simply understand the methods and procedures leading to each study's findings. It is sure that literature based on "evidence" that is not established in a systematic, objective, transparent manner is not empirical literature

4.4 Summary

Literature is the piece of work done alongside the theme. Reviewing those literature is the activity to understand the others contribution to the relevant field. By reviewing others scholarly contribution helps researcher to familiar with the pertinent theme of the study. Therefore, before to begin the research process, scholar must review the past literature in order to grasp the knowledge comprehensively. Due to that, researcher would become expert in the related field off study and he would able to contribute to the fresh knowledge to the relevant field of the research. This piece of work consist meaning of literature review along with major types of the literature review. Next, it explains function of literature review, then summary followed by theoretical and empirical literature review.

References

Connelly, L. (2014). Use of theoretical frameworks in research. *Medsurg Nursing: Official Journal of the Academy of Medical-Surgical Nurses, 23*, 187-188. Retrieved from http:// www.medsurgnursing.net/cgi-bin/WebObjects/MSNJournal.woa

de Souza.M.T, d. S. (2010). Integrative review: What is it? How to do it? *Einstein (16794508), 08*(01), 102-106.

Dubin, R. (1978). Theory building (Rev ed.). *NY: Free Press*.

Getthesis. (2019). *Get-Thesis*. Retrieved 01 15, 2020, from www.get-thesi.com: https://get-thesis.com/blog/writing-literature-review-guide,2019.01.20

Hart, C. (1998). Doing a Literaure Review. *SAGE*.

John R. Turner, R. B. (2018). Theoretical Literature Review : Tracing Life cycle of a theory and its Verified and Falsified Statement. *Human Resource Development Review*, 34-61. doi:10.1177/1534484317749680

Lynham, S. A. (2002a). The general method of theory-building research in applied disciplines. *Advances in Developing Human Resources*, 221-241. doi:10.1177/1523422302043002

Mark Sounders, P. L. (2009). *Reserch Methods for Business Students*. UK: Pearson Education Limited.

Merriam, S. B. (2000). A guide to research for educators and trainers of adults. *Malabar, FL: Krieger, 02*.

Merriam.SB, & L, S. E. (2000). A guide to research for educators and trainers of adults Malabar,. *FL: Krieger*.

Pitt, M. J. (2016). *What-is-the-function-of-literature-review-and-how-does-it-help-the-reader*. Retrieved from www.quora.com: Answered May 29, 2016 https://www.quora.com/What-is-the-function-of-literature-review-and-how-does-it-help-the-reader

Pressbooks, O. (2020). *ohiostate.pressbooks.pub*. Retrieved 01 28, 2020, from
www.ohiostate.pressbooks.pub:
https://ohiostate.pressbooks.pub/swk3401/chapter/chapter-3-what-is-empirical-
literature-where-can-it-be-found/

Schrijven. (2020). *schrijven*. Retrieved 01 23, 2020, from www.schrijven.ugent.be:
http://www.schrijven.ugent.be/node/439

Singh, Y. K. (2006). *Fundamendal of Research Methodology and Statistics.* New Delhi:
NEW AGE INTERNATIONAL (P) LIMITED, PUBLISHERS.

Tonntte.S, Maria.S, Rocco, & Plakhotnik. (2000). Literature Reviews, Conceptual
Frameworks, and TheoreticTerms, Functions, and Distinctionsal Frameworks. *Human
Resource Development Review, 08*(01), 120-150. doi:DOI: 10.1177/

Tranfield, D. a. (2004). Linking theory to practice: a grand challenge for management reserch
in 21st Century. *Organization Management Journal,, 01*(01), 10-14.

Uma Sekaran, R. B. (2013). *Research Methods for Business* (Vol. 7). UK: John Wiley &
Sons Ltd.

Uyangoda, J. (2018). *Wrting Reserch Proposal in the Social sciences and Humanities.*
Colombo: Social Scientists' Association.